P.S.

I Love You

*a collection of
God's love letters
to you*

CARL MILLER

TATE PUBLISHING, LLC

Published in the United States of America
by Tate Publishing, LLC
127 East Trade Center Terrace
Mustang, OK 73064
(888) 361-9473

ISBN: 1-9332903-3-1

DEDICATION

To my parents, Walter and Peggy Miller, of Plankinton, South Dakota, who brought me into the world and who have brought me up in the "nurture and admonition of the Lord."

Also to my dear wife, Mere Lyn, for all her support and encouragement.

I also proudly dedicate this book to my children, David and Becky, the next generation.

Foreword

By Rev. Ernest Gerike

People sometimes experience devotions (private prayer times) which are not quite complete. Something vital is missing. They fail to allow time for God to speak. As we talk with God in prayer, He is anxious and eager to speak to us. Sometimes we do not give Him the opportunity.

Dear Reader, if you have ever found this to be your problem, then praise the Lord for Carl Herman Miller's book: "P.S. I Love You"! From the loving, pastoral heart of this writer come letters which include spaces for the reader's name. The letters really are from God! Thus, God the Father, God the Son (Jesus), and God the Holy Spirit speak directly to the reader. As you read, you will sense the warm love of God reaching out to you.

A glance at the index will show the letters may be found in twenty one different books of the Bible. It is also worth noting the topics relate to every-day living. Here are some examples: "Confidence," "Fear," "Peace of Mind," "Identity," "You Are Special," "Life's Purpose," Overcoming Temptations," and "Good Decisions."

In writing this book, Pastor Miller has rendered a great favor for all of us.

Read and be personally blessed!

P.S. It really is Personalized Scripture.

Preface

Nearly everyone enjoys letters, especially from someone who loves them very much.

This book is in the form of short letters; P.S.- Personalized Scripture, adapted from God's word for you. It becomes personal as you put your own name in the blank lines.

God personally involves Himself in your life. He cares deeply about you as you will see through these letters.

~ Carl Miller

FROM US TO YOU

II Thessalonians 2: 13-17

Dear_____, We really love you. Before you were born, We chose you to be made holy by the Holy Spirit in order for you to believe the Truth (Us) so We could glorify you in giving you eternal life with Us. That has and is happening to you. We are just glad you are here at this time in history.

_____, our love to you is deep and will last forever, so the comfort and security you receive is also forever. This gives you confidence, an inner radiance and strength to do and say everything that is good.

_____, as We watch over you and work with you, We want to say we are very proud to have you as Our child.

Love you _____

God, your Father and Jesus Christ.

WALKING TOGETHER

Luke 15:8-10

_____, this is another very important day that we walk together. _____, you know that sin, the breaking of any of the Ten Commandments, hurts Me and also you. Having sinned is like being lost and not knowing how to get home, to be secure and happy again.

_____, it's important for you then, to tell Me your sins and be sorry for them. Do you know how it makes Me feel when you are sorry for them? I'm happy, I rejoice and so do all the angels in heaven. This, in turn, makes you happy to know how much I love you; that I forgive all your sins every day. I clothe you with My holiness, glory and love.

Jesus

CONFIDENCE

Psalm 18:28-30

_____, let Me continue to light up your life with My Word. Then you will have the confidence to face problems and overcome them with Me.

My way is perfect for you _____, and the promises in My Word are real and continue to come true for you. Two promises are: 1) I will always be your God and as you come to Me - you will always be secure in My power, and 2) I will protect and defend you every day of your life.

Loving you _____,

God

SAFEGUARD YOUR LIFE

Psalm 119:9-16

_____, with all the temptations and pressures in life; a young man once asked Me how to keep his way of life pure. My advice to young David and to you, young or old, is to safeguard your life with My Word. Seek Me with your whole heart and mind. Don't let yourself wander from My Commandments, but lay up My Word in your heart so you may not sin against Me and also hurt yourself.

Meditate and fix your eyes _____, on My ways. Rejoice in My Word as I rejoice in you.

My peace be with you,

God

GOD, MY FRIEND

Psalm 25:12-14

Dear _____, how many true friends do you have? How many really care for you every day of your life? Jesus knew what it was like to be friendless. At one point even His disciples ran away from Him. _____, I was Jesus' true friend in love all the time. My Words and love to Jesus made Him strong.

_____, I am your friend, too. I loved you even before you were born. Look at Me _____. Be aware of My Almighty power and love. I will teach you the way you must choose in life and in doing so you will enjoy the many good things I give. If you have children, they also will benefit from your looking to Me for life and salvation. Fear Me above everything else in the world and you will realize what a tremendous Friend I am to you.

Loving you,

God

13

SATISFYING

John 6:27-35

Dear _____, this is your Lord Jesus speaking. I see people working very hard for things that won't last. That's frustrating. In a time when the world is changing so rapidly, work for the "food", the relationship that will remain forever. I give you that food.

You have many needs. I have come to satisfy them. I am the bread of life. Keep coming to Me; hearing My Words to you. Believe Me and continue receiving Me into your life and you will never experience the painful hunger and thirst of your inmost needs going unmet.

I love you very deeply,

Jesus

LIFE'S PURPOSE

Romans 6:10-11

_____, why are you alive? Who are you living for? I want to help you answer these questions by giving you a pattern and purpose I follow in My life.

When I died on the cross for all of your sins your forgiveness was complete. As you accept My forgiveness, you are cleansed by My blood. I will never die again. So the life I now live, I live eternally for God My Father. You _____, because of your faith are with Me. Therefore think of yourself as having no life toward sin, but being alive and living for God your Father. That is, living with a purpose and glory. I know - I joyfully walked this earth, always living for God My Father.

Live in My Love _____,

Jesus

15

RAINBOW OF LOVE

Genesis 9:12-17

_____, when you see a rainbow, do you know what it means? It is a sign of the promise I made with Noah and his family after the Flood, and also with you; a promise to never again destroy all living beings on the earth by means of a flood. The rainbow is a sign of my promise to you, that will last forever. The rainbow, in all its splendor, is also a sign that I, your God, am in control of this world for you. It shows My glory, power and ever-living presence with you.

Rest easy in My arms _____,

God

TREASURES

I John 5:14-15

_____, the vast storehouse of treasures and blessings I have for you is limitless. If you want a stronger faith, increased confidence or more joy, love and peace in your life, just ask for it. I listen enthusiastically to your requests, because I love enriching your life with My many blessings.

Know this _____., when you ask for something that I want you to have, expect to receive it and you will. For instance, if you want more confidence, ask Me for it and then receive it through My Word, the Bible. Take note of what I've done for you in the past, am doing for you now and will be doing for you in the future. Note how many times I'm standing with you. Notice how all of this makes you feel and think. Then, discover you have what you asked for - more confidence.

Joy and peace to you,

Jesus

AT HOME WITH GOD

II Corinthians 6:14-18

Dear _____, you are a temple of the living God. As I have said before, I will live and walk with you. I am your God and you are My child. Therefore, don't follow people who don't believe in Me. Don't be a partner in doing wrong. Come away from such people and their evil ways and I will joyfully welcome you. I am your Father and you, with other believers in Jesus Christ, are My dear sons and daughters.

I love you deeply _____,

God

BORN FROM ABOVE

Romans 6:3-6

_____, I've noticed that whenever you got anything new, you were very proud of it. If it was worth it, the cost did not seem to matter.

_____, did you know that by your being baptized, you are brand new today? You are absolutely beautiful! When you were baptized, your old sin-loving self was crucified with Me on the cross so it could be destroyed. That cost a lot, but you are worth it. You were buried with Me by baptism into death, so, as I was raised from the dead, you, too, by My power can walk in newness of life every day. You are now free from the power of sin and Satan. Your sins are forgiven every day. In Me, you are new, powerful, and valuable. We are together now, and will be even closer when I return to receive you to Myself.

I love you _____,

Jesus

YOU ARE PRICELESS

I Thessalonians 5:23-24

_____, this is God your Father. Since there is peace between us by way of your sins being washed away at the cross, I want to continue keeping you holy. I want your whole life and body sound, without a fault, when your Lord Jesus returns. I will do that for you. You can depend on what I say. I have called you to be My very own. You're too valuable for My ministry to let anything come between us.

I love you _____, very much,

God

YOUR INHERITANCE

Romans 8:18-19

_____, what if you were suffering and someone said you would inherit ten million dollars next week? How important would that suffering be? What would you be thinking about most? The inheritance would probably affect your thinking and way of life.

_____, the tremendous, earth-shaking glory I will give to you is worth more than everything in this whole wide world. Even the creation is waiting expectantly to see the magnificent glory that you will have with all other believers in Me.

_____, let your suffering and hurt as a Christian be swallowed up by My love to you and the kingly glory coming your way, as I return in the near future.

Let your mind rest on this.

Jesus

A THANKFUL HEART

Luke 17:16-19

_____, I've done many wonderful things in your life. Do you know what I've done today for you? How often do you thank Me for loving you, for making you My very special person in the world?

Like the healed leper, realizing what I had done for him, he came back praising and thanking Me. May this also be your response. Let praise and thankfulness come as a result of receiving and being aware of the blessings I give to you. This in turn, leads to a more positive outlook on life and yourself.

Many blessings to you _____,

Jesus

ALL THE WAY

Romans 12:1-2

_____, hope this has been a super week for you. I died on the cross for the forgiveness of all your sins and also those who sinned against you. I want to fill you with my joy, love, and peace. Trouble is, My child, you've been holding out on Me at times. You give part of yourself to Me, but you give a part of yourself to the world; believing what they say about you. Come, now, I've made My choice, My total commitment to you. Give yourself completely to Me. You are able to do that by allowing your mind to be daily renewed by My Word of Truth. Then you will be able to test things to be sure they are good, pleasing and perfect - what I want for you.

I love you, _____,

Jesus

PEACE OF MIND

Matthew 11:28-30

_____, come to Me. Come with all your worries, problems, heartaches. Come with your sins, guilt and confusion about life. Come with your "rushing to and fro". Come and I, Jesus Christ your Lord, will give you rest through My Word.

Take instead what I give to you and learn from Me - I am gentle and humble minded - then you will find your rest. What I give you to carry is easy and light. Come _____, we walk together in peace and strength.

With an overflowing love to you,

_____,

Jesus

WISDOM

I Kings 3:5-12

_____, hope your week is going well. What would you like to have? I asked King Solomon that. Know what he asked for? It wasn't riches, a long life or death of his enemies. Solomon asked that his heart and mind know how to obey Me and be able to understand what is good and bad. I gave him intelligence, understanding and also riches and honor he did not ask for.

_____, you need to also obey Me, and in doing that, not only will you understand what is good and what is evil, but, will be walking with your head held high, proudly knowing you act like a king as you use My Word.

I love you,_____,

God

CONFIDENT LIVING

Romans 8:28

_____, there are so many great things I want to tell you to help you live life successfully and confidently. I've called you by My Word. As you joyfully continue to love me with all your heart, I promise to work good out of everything that happens in your life.

Love and Peace,

Jesus Christ

BEAUTIFUL EXCHANGE

Romans 5:6-11

_____, I really enjoy talking with you. You're a good listener. Do you remember a time when you felt weak, confused, anxious and kind of lost in knowing what to do or think? Then, those feelings sometimes led you to do things that hurt others, including yourself. You also hurt Me. It hurt God, your Father, too. We knew that no matter how hard you tried, you would never be able to stop hurting us and yourself. So, I gladly and willingly came to earth and went to the cross to suffer and die for all your sins - abolishing them completely.

_____, in place of weakness, I gave you my strength, my Truth to replace confusion, and peace to calm your anxious heart. I've found you; you'll never be lost again. I'll never let you go. I've given you My life, eternal life. Do you know what that means? It means we'll love each other and celebrate our new relationship forever and ever. I'm so happy we're together, and so is God, your Father.

Jesus Christ

STANDING WITH YOU

Psalm 121

_____, this is God. I'll speak to you today through David of the Old Testament:

"_____, when you need help, where do you go? What do you do? For me, I will lift up mine eyes, for my help comes from the Lord who made heaven and earth. _____, God will keep you firm and steady - He's always awake for you, calmly standing with you, as He always has for me. The Lord is your keeper and comforter. He stands guard over your precious life.

The Lord your God can keep your life from the power of evil. He will make you secure and strong in your going out and your coming in from this time forth and for evermore."

David, a servant of God

CONTENTMENT

Romans 4:24-5:1

_____, this is your Heavenly Father speaking. Remember when Jesus was put to death? That happened so by your sins being forgiven, you could feel good about Me and happy toward yourself. Jesus your Lord also rose from the dead so you wouldn't be afraid of death. As you believe in Jesus and accept what He did for you, I joyfully accept you into My loving arms. Listen _____, since I accept you as My very special child, I also want to give you My peace. My peace will give you contentment and drive away any anxieties, because now we're a team.

I'm glad, _____, you're with Me. We're going to do a lot of great things together.

In deepest love,

Your Heavenly Father

YOU ARE SPECIAL

John 14:1-12

_____, this is Jesus speaking. Don't let your heart be troubled, in spite of what may be happening around you. Do you know what I'm doing for you? I am personally preparing a special place for you _____, and the rest of our Family in my Father's heavenly home. You believe in God, believe also in Me.

Something else _____,– I'll be coming back to see you and to take you to be with me, so that wherever I will be, you _____, can be with me; talking, sharing and loving each other forever. Hope you're excited about it as much as I am. I think about you a lot.

_____, I want our relationship to be super strong. I especially want to show you My Father. You've never seen such a loving Father as He is. It's very important for you to continue to listen to Me and obey Me. Follow Me and I will give you truth to make you wise and life eternal to make you secure in our relationship.

As you get to know me _____, real well, then you will also know My Father and our tremendous love for you.

_____, remember how great you thought I was on earth doing all those wonderful things for people? You wished you could be like me. I am going to give you power through My Word so that you will do works just as great and even greater works on earth than I did, because you trust in Me and follow My example. What do you think of that? Yes, I trust you with my power because my constant love to you will guide you in the right decisions. If you need anything, let me know, and I will give you what you need. I stand with you, supporting and encouraging you all the way. I love you.

Jesus Christ

STANDING PROUD

Romans 5:2

_____, I know it's tough for you in this world, but I want you to hold your head high, standing firm, being proud of who you are, My child, because my love for you _____ is so deep and strong! Oh, I'm so very proud of you. I'm going to share My glory and joy with you every day. I know we're going to have a beautiful day together. My peace be with you.

Jesus Christ

RENEWED STRENGTH

Isaiah 40:28-31

_____, I pay very close attention to everything you do and say. I am your Lord, the everlasting God, the Creator of this whole earth. I do not faint or grow weary. My understanding of you is unsearchable. I can give power to you when you are faint and strength when you feel weak. People who turn their back on Me shall grow weak; even youths shall faint, be weary and young men fall exhausted.

But _____, listen and obey My Words and I shall renew your strength. You shall rise with wings like eagles. You shall run for Me and not be weary. You shall walk for Me and not be faint. You are My special creation.

I love you,

God

REFRESHING

Isaiah 55:1-5

_____, this is God speaking. When you thirst for love, importance, or security, come to the refreshing waters of My Word. What I give is priceless, no money can buy it. I plan to glorify you with My love, show you how important you are by dying in your place on the Cross and make you secure in My Power. Therefore, _____, why spend your money for that which does not nourish you and work for that which does not satisfy? Listen closely to Me, feast on My Word and be delighted in your satisfaction. Come to Me, continue to hear Me that you may live the full life intended for you. Let My life fill your life to overflowing!

God

A PEACEFUL SLEEP

Romans 1:7

_____, hope you've had a very blessed week. You are My beloved child, special - I call you to be a saint, believing in Me as your Lord and Savior. As you go to sleep tonight, God your Father and I just want you to know we love you very much. May our peace, received by the forgiveness of your sins, calm and relax you as We watch over you tonight.

Jesus

SET FREE

John 8:28-32; 12:49-50

_____, have you ever felt like you were doing and saying many things, but wondered if it was all worth the effort? Ever feel trapped by the various voices of the world? _____, follow Me. Do what I did. I did only those things that My Father taught Me. I listened to Him a lot. As I obeyed Him, I received His approval and constant companionship. His truth gave Me power and security.

_____, listen to Me, (My Word), and you will have My approval and recognition as you do and say those things that please Me. Continue in My Word and you are My disciple indeed. You shall know the Truth _____, and this will set you free from the hurtful traps of the world.

Loving you,

Jesus

36

IDENTITY

Matthew 13:24-30

_____, Imagine you were wheat or weeds in a wheat field, what do you think you would be? If you saw yourself as "wheat" and all the weeds around you called you a "weed," would you believe it? How would you know for sure? _____, you are called many things in this world – some are true, some are false and destructive. How do you really know who you are?

Continue to listen to Me, _____, and I will not only tell you that I died for you to forgive your sins, but as you follow Me, I will also guard and protect your life eternally.

_____, you are My Chosen, beloved disciple. Your past, present and future is secure in My hands. When I return, the deceptive, destructive "weeds" of the world will be banished, but you will rejoice in My Heavenly Home I have prepared for you.

Jesus

TO WHOM DO YOU LISTEN?

John 12:42-43

_____, what do you like most - the praise of people or My praise? Does what other people say about you determine your words and actions or does what I say determine your life? Many love the praise of men more than My praise and thus refuse to confess Me in their life. I pray this is not so with you, for I love you deeply, _____.

Jesus

MANY BLESSINGS

Genesis 12:1

_____, this is God speaking. Hope you've seen and felt My blessings upon you this week. _____, I spoke to Abraham and directed his life by My Word. I desire to direct your life also by My Word in the Bible. Abraham could have chosen to disobey me because it was not easy to do something he had not done before. Abraham obeyed Me though, and was blessed many times over.

_____, it may not be easy for you always to obey Me by following Jesus Christ by faith, not sight. Yet if you obey My Word, I promise rich blessings will come into your life. Listen and obey then, not because of the blessings, but because I am your God who loves you deeply. I have a plan for your life.

Many blessings to you _____,

God

PLANNED FOR, PRECIOUS

Isaiah 43:1-5, 10

_____, how has your week been? Have you ever wondered how you came to be on this earth? Some may say it just happened that way – it was just chance. I say that I planned for you to be on this earth at this time in history. I personally created and formed you. I purchased you by the blood of Jesus Christ and called you, _____, to be My very own.

Yes, as you go through life and its problems, I will be with you. No matter what happens, nothing shall overwhelm you. The roaring evil fire of this world shall not overtake you because I am the LORD YOUR GOD. _____, you are precious in My eyes, honored and I love you. Don't ever be afraid of anything - for I am with you.

Your loving, powerful God

GOOD DECISIONS

Colossians 3:15

_____, you make many decisions every day. You want them to be right. I'll help you. When you have a decision to make, first remember the peace I give to you every day by forgiving your sins. Let your mind be calm and restful in My warm, secure peace. Then, know I called you, along with all other believers in Me, as one body. Don't let anything tear down your Christian faith.

_____, thank Me for the many expressions of love I give to you every day. List what they are. This will help you see how valuable and precious you are to Me. Now, with these thoughts, make your decision.

Jesus

CELEBRATE

Colossians 3:16-17

_____, I hope this week has been a blessing for you. Have you noticed My presence? I talk to you, but it's very important for My Word to live and be celebrated in your life – then you can joyfully teach people about Me.

With your heart filled with thankfulness by My Word (Me), you also discover yourself singing songs of praise to Me. _____, in everything you do or say, do it in My Name and by Me give thanks to God your Father. We both love you very much.

Jesus

YOU ARE SUCCESSFUL

I John 4:4

_____, do not believe everything you hear. Test what you hear against My Word. There are many false prophets in the world who could make you feel confused. But by your faith in Me, you are secure, as My child in My Family. You have won a victory over these deceptive, self-centered people. The reason for the victory is because He (Jesus Christ), who is in you, is greater than he (Satan), who is in the world. _____, you are a success through Me.

God

MORE THAN A KERNEL

John 12:23-26

_____, how have you been? Imagine, if you will, that you are a kernel of corn. Many other kernels try to get you to join their cause and join them in a fight for their "rights" in a kernel campaign. You hear slogans like "The joy of being and remaining a kernel," and "The way to happiness as a kernel." You sense that there are a lot of unhappy kernels.

Then you hear another voice. You recognize it as the one who created you. He says: "Give yourself to Me as a living sacrifice. You must die to your old ideas of being just a kernel. You are created to be much more, to produce fruit and bring forth happiness and joy, not just to others, but to yourself." _____, as you give your life over to Me completely and follow Me in My Word, you are given eternal life. My Father will personally honor you for serving Me. Your happy, fulfilled, real life is found through Me.

Love you _____,

Jesus

STANDING BEFORE GOD

Psalm 119:161-168

_____, imagine that you are standing before Me saying the following words: "Father, I just wanted to talk with you and tell you what I'm thinking and feeling. As you know, my whole life is open to your loving eye of concern for me. Sometimes I feel like I'm being chased away from You, pressured to conform to the ways of a cold, non-caring, restless world. I hear lies and distortions about myself and others. I hate those things! If it wasn't for You and Your Word of Truth, I'd probably believe those lies.

But, Father, Your Word gives me strength and confidence. I love your teachings and am delighted with the Words you speak to me. It's like receiving a treasure chest filled with precious gems and jewels that I may wear. I remember what You say and how You feel towards me. You make me very happy. Thank you Father for listening to me. I surely do love You!"

I love you, too, _____,

Your Father

PARABLES

Matthew 13:13-16

_____, have you ever known some-
one who heard and saw you speaking, but they never
understood what you meant? Many people are like
that towards Me. They hear My Words, but quickly
leave thinking they know it all. To you, _____,
because you stay and listen to the meaning behind My
Words, you understand Me and yourself better. My
Word is like a healing medicine to you, while to others who have left Me, only parables remain. You are
blessed because your eyes see and your ears hear Me
clearly.

Joyfully loving you, _____,

Jesus

YOU ARE RICH

Philippians 4:19-20

_____, I hope you've been blessed this week. Just a thought for you, but very important. Whenever you feel you need something, tell Me what it is and I promise to fulfill your needs according to all my glorious riches that are all a part of your inheritance. You are indeed a very rich person, _____, because of our strong relationship of love. I am proud of you. You give glory to God.

Jesus

THE SUCCESSFUL WAY

Proverbs 16:2-3

_____, how are things going for you? I know that you'd like to think everything you do is the best. I will help you. Tell Me your true intentions and attitude in what you plan to do. In using My Word as a standard, you will know if your ways are also My Ways, and therefore the best.

_____, save yourself a lot of frustration, failure and fatigue by first entrusting your work and plans to Me for review. Then, with My stamp of approval, your plan will succeed and be fulfilled.

_____, as our relationship continues in My Word every day, you will discover yourself talking and acting more like Me. You will find yourself more confident and being more successful as our relationship becomes stronger.

I love you,

God

OUR CLOSE RELATIONSHIP

Romans 5:3-5

_____, I am glad we can talk together. As you rejoice in our close relationship you will have more confidence in what we are doing together. You can also rejoice in your problems, because you can use my wisdom and strength to resolve them. You will also discover the amazing patience you have.

Not only that, _____, but, having successful experiences in working through problems will increase your confidence in My ability to help you. You will never have to doubt your confidence and leadership capabilities because the love of God is always being given to you by the Holy Spirit.

Jesus

DIVINE LOVE

I Corinthians 13:4-8

_____, allow Me, your Lord Jesus Christ, to describe what My love to you is like. May this also describe your love:

- •I am patient and understanding with you.
- •I am kind to you.
- •I never compare you with others.
- •I don't brag about Myself.
- •I do only that which uplifts our relationship.
- •I am not selfish.
- •I respond to your sins not with angry revenge, but with loving forgiveness.
- •I help you and am happy as you follow the Truth of My Word.
- •I bear and endure everything for you, even death, so that you may live eternally.

My love for you never dies _____ Come, let us continue to walk together; My hand holding yours.

Love, peace, joy,

Jesus

I AM YOUR GOD

Psalm 100:1-5

My precious_____, this is the Lord your God. I want you to know I am not only the Lord your God, but I personally made you. You are My adopted child through Jesus Christ. You are living in the world I created for you.

Therefore, _____, serve Me with gladness and with a song in your heart. Come to Me with thanksgiving, praise and thanks. Compliment Me for all I'm doing for you, for My goodness, mercy and truth that endures to all generations.

Love you, _____,

God

WORKING THROUGH YOU

Hebrews 13:21

_____, I will give you every good thing you need so that you are able to do what I want you to do. Do you know what pleases Me _____ _____? It is when you allow Me to work in you through Jesus Christ. You discover that it is also pleasing to you!

As Christ does magnificent works through you, give Me the glory forever and ever. Amen.

Giving you abundant life _____,

God

TREMENDOUS POTENTIAL

Matthew 14:13-21

_____, hope you have been aware of My continual presence with you this week. You are very important to Me. You are very important to your family and neighbors. What you have to give may seem little in your eyes. Kind of like the disciples with their five loaves of bread and two fish in face of over 5,000 people.

I say to you what I said to them, "Bring to Me what you have - talents, ability, personality, your whole self so I may bless them and use them in My way." Allow Me to bless other people through you. Your talents and ministry to others will be multiplied. You'll be surprised at how rich you are in Me.

Come to Me, _____, let Me bless you – your heart, mind and soul. Go forth My child and let yourself be a continual blessing to your family and neighbors.

Love you richly, _____,

Jesus

JOYFUL LISTENER

Matthew 16:13-17

_____, hope you have had a good week. Who do you say I am? Who am I to you? Why do you think I keep talking to you and loving you? Listen to the "world" and they, speaking in their darkness, will say many things. Who do you say I am? If you say: "You are the Christ, the Savior, the Son of the Living God," then you have been listening well, for My Father in heaven has revealed this to you.

Continue to follow Me, _____, as you joyfully live your life in Me.

Loving you tenderly, _____,

Jesus

FEAR — DEFEATED

Exodus 14:13-14

_____, I understand that certain things really get you down. You are not sure whether you will be able to handle them. Kind of like how the Old Testament Israelites felt when the Egyptians were going to overtake them.

_____, as I told them, I tell you - do not be afraid. Just stand still and see how I am going to take you through this day and week. Listen to My Word, _____, I am fighting for you. As you know, I saved the Israelites by My Word as the Red Sea was miraculously divided allowing them to walk across it on dry land. MY WORD, being active in your heart and mind also defeats the every day enemies that arise. GO in My power and love.

God

OVERCOMING TEMPTATIONS

I Corinthians 10:13

_____, I know you are tempted to say or do things that are against My will. I want you to know how I can help you. First, your temptations to evil will be those that are common to mankind. Second, I am faithful to My love for you and I will not let you be tempted beyond your strength, but with the temptation will provide the way to escape; to overcome it. The way is through a close relationship of love with Me and sharing our thoughts and feelings with each other. My Word of truth shall be your strength.

I hold you close with My love,

Jesus

GOD'S WORD — FOR YOU

II Timothy 3:16

_____, I would like you to know the source and purpose of My Word as you hear and read it in the Old and New Testament. All scripture, every word, is given by Me. It is useful for teaching you, for showing you what is wrong, and for your improvement and training in right living, so that you may be ready and equipped for every good work I give you.

_____, I share My Word of Life with you because I love you. I'm listening to your thoughts and feelings also.

Love and life,

God

CHOSEN, CALLED TO GLORY

II Thessalonians 2:13-17

_____, My beloved _____,
I have chosen you from the beginning to be made holy
by the Spirit, to believe the Truth and so to be saved.
That is why I called you by My Word. I want you to
have the glory of your Lord Jesus Christ.

Cling to My Word, _____, for your
Lord Jesus Christ and God your Father love you and
give you everlasting comfort and good hope by our
continuous grace. _____, I will inwardly
comfort your heart and mind and establish you in
every good word and work.

Loving you,

God

THE SECRET TO LOVING

1 John 4:7-12

_____, have you ever wished you could love others more than you do? Here is how. A person who doesn't love with My kind of pure, deep love doesn't know Me because I am love. The secret to loving is in knowing Me and receiving My love. I've shown you My love, _____, by sending My Son Jesus Christ to die for your sins. Yes, you are very important to Me. Allow Jesus to give you Himself through the Word day after day and you will experience My deep and abiding love to you. As you then love others with My overflowing love, you will know that you are indeed My beloved child.

God

YOU ARE VALUABLE

Matthew 10:28-33

_____, your life is a witness to other people. If you acknowledge Me before others, I will acknowledge you to My Father in heaven. If anyone denies Me before others, him will I deny before My Father.

_____, don't be afraid of what others do to you physically, because they cannot harm you spiritually. Fear him who can destroy you physically and spiritually in hell. _____, I am your refuge and strength. You are extremely valuable to Me, priceless! I even know how many hairs are on your head. I will lead you through life.

I love you, _____,

Jesus

LIFE OVER DEATH

Romans 5:12, 15-17

_____, have you ever wondered why people die? One man, Adam, brought sin into the world and his sin brought death. Now because all have sinned, death spread to all people. I hate death, but I do love you so I died and was punished in your place for all your sins. _____, that (which) means I have given you the gift of eternal life because I rose from the dead, defeating the power of death and sin.

Yes, death was once a fearful king, but now I, Jesus Christ, empower you to live on past death and be with Me. Spiritually, you will always be with Me. Even when physical death comes, it will be but a sleep until I return and give you a spiritual body. This will all happen as you continue to believe in Me and My Word.

Love you,

Jesus

RELATIONSHIPS

Romans 12:20-21

_____, everyone seems to have enemies. I know I did. You probably know people too, who are not very kind to you. Want to know how to handle them? Come closer. If that person ever needs something, try to help meet that need. Smile, compliment and praise something good in him. In doing that, he will be ashamed of his own lack of kindness and will possibly treat you better than ever before.

In this way, _____, you don't let evil conquer you, but rather overcome the evil of others by being good to them.

My richest blessing to you, _____,

Jesus

HOME

Philippians 3:20-21

_____, where is home for you? As you believe in Me as your Lord and Savior, your real, eternal home is with Me - in the Kingdom of God. Since I am king and I have personally called you by My Word to serve Me, be looking to Me with your whole heart and mind.

_____, I rejoice over you and look forward to the day when I shall return in all glory and power to change your body so it will be like My glorious body. You are strong and safe in My power, _____, for all things in heaven and earth are subject unto Me.

To My beloved, _____,

Jesus

DIVINE SHEPHERD

Psalm 23

Dear _____, this is Jesus your Lord speaking. I am your Shepherd. In Me you have everything you need. I often make you stop, lie down, and reflect on what I'm doing for you. _____, I lead you to the refreshing water of My Word so you can rest. I lead you to see your sins forgiven, to be at peace with God and yourself, on the path of being always set right, with Me.

_____, even in times of confusion, difficulty or weakness, you will fear no harm, because I am with you My power and love give you courage. We can have a great time – even enjoy a banquet prepared right in front of our enemies. You see, _____ _____, My power has defeated them. When you are hurt, I hold you close, having chosen you as My beloved child. My kindness and love will be with you all your life and you will live in My house forever.

Love you, _____,

Jesus

MY WORD IS VICTORY

Jeremiah 20:7-13

_____, you say you want to follow Me. People may laugh at you. When you speak My Word, you may not be "popular" anymore; instead you may be made fun of. Are you ready for that?

When My Word is like a burning fire in your heart compelling you to speak, people may reject and hate you. But, _____, I the Lord your God will fight your battles, so that those who pressure you will never win, because you have My personal protection. My powerful Word is your victory.

_____, live in My Word and speak it. Don't worry, I'll fight your battles. You can sing praises to Me while suffering and being ridiculed, because like Jesus on the cross, you know the final outcome is not defeat, but Victory.

Rejoice, _____, I love you strongly.

God

FOCUS ON ME

Matthew 14:22-33

_____, this is Jesus. You can do great works for Me or little or none at all, depending on your choice of focus for your life. If you consciously focus your life on Me, great things happen, such as when Peter walked on water, but when his attention shifted away from Me to the wind and water, he became afraid and began to sink.

_____, you must daily make that choice. Focus, believe in Me and My Words to you, and you will mentally and emotionally rise above the turmoil of the world, even though you may physically be in the midst of it. The other choice is to focus on other things and people. Then, fear and distortions come. You begin to sink - mentally, emotionally and physically. _____, you are making that first choice every day as you hear My Word and believe it.

I rejoice in you, _____,

Jesus

HUMBLED — EXALTED

Philippians 2:5-11

_____, I understand many recognize Me as being true God, but they find it hard to accept the fact I was true Man, and that they can be like Me. How about you? Do you accept Me as your pattern for life? _____, I emptied Myself of the powers of God. I became a servant, was always obedient to the loving will of My Father in heaven, and humbled Myself til I died on the cross for your sins. I was like you in every way as a human being except that I was not born a sinner. Even though I could have disobeyed My Father, I did not do so, but chose to rely on His power to help Me. _____, rely on Me to help you. Follow Me and listen to My Word, and as I was exalted as Lord over heaven and earth, so also you shall be exalted in glory when I return.

Love you, _____,

Jesus

GOLIATH

I Samuel 17:22-24, 40-50

_____, this is David from the Old Testament. Have you ever lost courage, been afraid, then ran away from a situation that needed your attention? If so, the men of Israel were like that when they faced the giant Goliath. Nobody wanted to fight him even though he despised God. Well, as you know, I faced Goliath with only a stick, five small stones and a sling shot. Goliath had armor on; a sword, spear and javelin. I defeated this enemy of God with a single shot. I had confidence and courage because I knew the Lord was with me. He is mightier than all the enemies you'll ever have.

Who or what is the "Goliath" in your life? Walk up to it, face it, and overcome it by the power of the Lord and His Word. Let God give you the confidence and courage you need through His mighty Word.

Love,

David

MY WORD IS TRUTH

John 17:17-19

_____, I desire to make you holy. I do it by means of the Truth. My Word is Truth. As My Father sent Me into the world, I also send you as My disciple into the world.

_____, I gave My life for you on the cross. I continue to give you Myself through My Word. My blood washes away all your sins. Rejoice in Me! My Truth shall guide you through this troubled world. May this be a very blessed week for you.

I care for you, _____,

Jesus

LIVE IN MY LOVE

Ephesians 5:1-2, 8-10

_____, as My dear child, try to be like Me. Live in my love as I have loved you and gave Myself for you on the cross as a fragrant offering and sacrifice to God. Once, _____, you were lost in darkness, but now you are full of light through Me. Live then, reflecting the love, forgiveness and joy that gracefully flows through you. This light of My Word produces everything good, righteous and true. Therefore test things by My Word to see if they please Me. If they please Me, _____, then you have My blessing which makes you happy.

Loving you,

Jesus

SCRIPTURE INDEX

I Thessalonians 5:23-24---You Are Priceless
II Thessalonians 2:13-17---Chosen, Called To Glory
II Timothy 3:16---God's Word – For You
Hebrews 13:21---Working Through You
I John 4:4---You Are Successful
I John 4:7-12---Secret To Loving
I John 5:14-15---Treasures

Contact Carl Miller
or order more copies of this book at

TATE PUBLISHING, LLC

127 East Trade Center Terrace
Mustang, Oklahoma 73064

(888) 361 - 9473

Tate Publishing, LLC

www.tatepublishing.com